Indefinable Pursuit

Radhika Verma

INDIA • SINGAPORE • MALAYSIA

ISBN

Hardcase 979-8-89026-485-5
Paperback 979-8-88909-889-8

Art work by - Mr. Keshav Roy
Proofread by - Renu Roy

Dedication

To the journey of life that taught me a lot,
That which was lost and blessed for all that one has got,
Those who walked away when time got rough,
Thanking them now for making the soul so tough,
A dedication to the mysteries of being,
As life unfolds to all not yet seen......

Contents

1

Memories

Life is a journey through fragrant memories,
Like bunches of flowers that bloom in our heart,
They leave a sweet fragrance of the cherished moment's right from the start,
Memories, some good and others bad,
They bring a smile on the face or make us extremely sad,
A fine deed is something we always treasure,
The joy felt is beyond measure,
The loss of a dear one haunts our memory for many years,
Fills the soul with grief and fills the eyes with tears,
The beauty of life is that it carries on from the beginning till the end,
Some memories sweet as honey and some like broken buttons we can not mend...

2

Man is What He Emotionally is

A person may look hard as rock or soft as cotton,
The kind we always remember or one who can be easily forgotten,
One may seem like a thorn on a rose,
Difficult to penetrate into, a negative aura they may dispose,
Sentiments and emotions difficult to comprehend,
In the materialistic world of today selfish seems like the trend,
Karmas is what carry one far,
In the vicious circle of life, deeds are always at par,
Values and humanity in a person are what must really matter,
As the rest of the emotions like dry seeds everywhere scatter.

3

Thoughts are the Culprit

Thoughts are the culprit for every step we take,
Responsible for most of the decisions in we make,
It is easier for negative thoughts to take over our mind,
In a jumble of emotions often ourselves we find,
A good thought makes us judicious and full of affection,
We must not let thoughts rule us as they are mere self studies reflections,
Thoughts come and go at the speed of lightening and thunder,
Sometimes stable and at times leave us in a state of wonder,
Preconceived notions and building new thoughts all along,
A never ending saga and the magic of thoughts life
carries on......

4

If

If our mind is entangled in pre conceived ideas and notions,

The consistent ripples on the surface of life like the mysterious ocean,

One may not understand life and its endless beauty,

As we start existing and not living life, it becomes like a mundane duty,

The power of discrimination is a tool which should be used for evolving,

Channelize the chakra of energies in a positive manner which helps in internal problem solving,

One must accept things around as they really seem,

Be realistic but in life one must have a vision and dream,

Like the warmth of the sun and the moonlit night,

Enjoy the simple things and do not let "if" take away
the light ...

5

Relationships

A relationship which takes many years of care to grow,

A misunderstanding and like a feather away it blows,

A constant process where the ego must not rule,

In a relationship an argument does not prove ones point,

It determines how desperate one is to prove a point,

Harmony is a practice one must try and swallow,

Relationships must be embedded in our soul and not be hollow,

Our strengths and weakness are legendary,

Relationships are as precious as vintage wine,

The value of them increases with time...

6

Forgiveness

Forgiveness is letting "what was " be gone,

A mistake at night one should try and forget at dawn,

Forgive and forget and be flexible towards thee,

Insecurity is nothing but the non acceptance of yourself as you really are,

Ill feelings do not carry an individual very far,

Have your principles in life but do not be inflexible,

Be humble so that to all one is acceptable,

In life one must take onus of their faults and mistakes,

Count ones blessings and avoid being responsible for someone's heart break...

7

Winds of Change

The winds of change on which we ride,
Like an ocean with the ever-changing tide,
An undying hope, an everlasting faith,
Like the angels were waiting at heaven's gate,
Possessed by the mysticism of the emotions,
A constant yet an inexpressible notion,
An innocent prayer like a newborn child,
Like an undiscovered place in the forest wild,
The integration of colors from which new ones evolve,
The puzzle of life which we try and solve,
The winds of change by which each one of us are orchestrated,
Living the moments which for us life has created...

8

Winter Blues

The mayhem and the winter blues,

The rustling winds, various tunes it construes,

The warm ray of the sun that makes the flowers bloom,

Enlightens the heart, takes away the gloom,

Like an unfinished story which had a heartwarming start,

As if the majestic rainbow was musing a color bright,

The dark sky, no moon in sight,

Yet the feeling stays engraved in the soul,

Like the strong blowing winds, hard to control

9

A Desire

A DESIRE TO SEE THE EMOTIONS SET FREE,
Let only peace your neighbor be,
A side where mentally, only joyous tunes you hears,
Where there is no room for any kind of fear,
The turbulence of life which makes the gates to love close,
Where lost is the fragrance of the beautiful rose,
A desire to see the clouds dancing in the rain,
I wish it washes away all your pain,
I wish for you to love your soul,
Break free and just let the heart control.

10

Gratitude

Gratitude is a mere recognition as a fact of living reality,
It is a recognition which cleanses all our inner negativity,
Gratitude leads to acceptance of others superiority,
It is an intense inner feeling of thankfulness by keeping aside inferiority,
Gratitude is born by living in facts,
It must be extended to everyone in need by selfless acts,
Gratitude is an attitude which helps us to appreciate people for what they are,
It leads to identification of others with no discrimination or bar,
Gratitude towards others gives them a sense of belongings and security,
In our heart emerges a sense of peace and serenity,
Gratitude should be an unbreakable knot that our heart and mind ties,
It should live in our heart and flow through our eyes.

11

You Are the Reason in Life, the Reason for Life

Sometimes like a twig in the storm you feel,
Sometimes our own emotions from ourselves we steal,
Like a kite that flies in the breeze so calm and composed,
Sometimes like a dry leaf which from the tree was disposed,
The support of illusionary arguments within,
Moments that make memories feel like a lifelong sin,
Nowhere to run, no place to hide,
The constant swim against the tide,
Until one day a person changes it all,
You know they will be there every time you fall,
They were the hope that existed in the heart,
They become the reason in life for a fresh start......

12

Love

True love is a touching of hearts and blending of souls,
In love every emotion our heart controls,
The soul becomes stable by becoming free,
Not restricting to force stability,
We are each one of us like angels with one wing,
Depending on one another for everything,
Love can only be given and not demanded,
It is only understanding and cannot be commanded,
A beautiful truth that comes with full devotion
The mind like a river hat looses itself in the wide ocean, when in love; always substitute the expecting with accepting......

13

Optimism

Optimism is like the light which guides us to our goal,
Pessimism is like the disease which contaminate our soul,
Optimism leads us into a world of success,
Pessimism demoralizes us and leaves us in distress,
An optimist fights challenges of life as they really are,
For a pessimist every goal seems like a destination too far,
If one feels discouraged just keep it in mind,
The motivation within oneself one finds,
Think like a winner for only then would one achieve,
All one has to do is focus and believe,
The oyster of life in which people come n go,
Some like precious pearls and others mere acquaintances good to know,
Be an optimist and obstacles are easily overcome,
Conviction and nothing would be left undone ...

14

The Dedication

The dedication of the rising sun every morning,
The musical tone of every bird singing,
The freshness of the dew on the wet grass,
The blooming of the beautiful flowers,
The softness of the feather of a bird,
The mystic feeling of every heart in the rain,
The purity of holy water, the dedication towards love one feels,
The soul embraces and the heart reveals.

15

Destiny

Destiny and man walk hand in hand,
Every step seems predestined,
Each day reveals a new chapter in life's book,
Before we leap one must always look,
One must not look down upon others and keep humanity aside,
As malice has a way of drowning one in and the true self one tends to hide,
A systematic approach to win life's race,
Hold on tu the composure no matter what we have to face,
One should hold our hands in graciousness for the time that goes by,
Thank lord for the moon n sun that majestically shines in the sky,
Never lose yourself esteem, never laugh at a lame,
As it would take a sec for lords magic wand to play destiny's game...

16

Selfless Deeds

One should try in life to follow selfless deeds,

Philanthropic acts not always catering to one's own needs,

A selfless act that brings joy to a needy is like a priceless treasure,

The intensity and value of which is beyond measure,

It is human nature to get carried away,

Try and work on the karma and not go mentally astray,

Evolution of the mind and the soul,

Selfless deeps as a part of existence one must try and behold,

A true winner is one who succeeds beyond one own expectations,

And be grateful for lord's precious creations ...

17

Time

A commodity that cannot be bought or sold,
More precious than the shining gold,
Priceless and for no one it waits,
A fair player that treats all the same at its courts gate,
The inestimable value of each second that goes by,
Time that elates us or makes us bitterly cry,
The flavors of life that we taste bit by bit,
Never waste time and make the most of it,
Loss which can be cured only with time,
Often ourselves in a dilemma of various natures we find,
Aim to be priceless and boundless like time,
And oneself striving harder in life one finds...

18

Rise in Love not Fall in Love

A mystifying emotion two people share,

Separation which becomes difficult to bear,

A time when the heart if completely at par,

Thoughts which keep the mind preoccupied at every hour,

Faith and belief are what we follow,

All else seems pointless and logic hollow,

One should rise in love as it is endearing,

A boundless ocean to be conquered without fearing,

Rise in love and the ultimate goal is to cross every hurdle that comes ones way,

Just be grateful to rise in love every passing day.

19

Believe

If we believe in ourselves no obstacle can come our way,
One should count your blessing for the rising sun
each day,
Confidence of the bright blue sky,
That canopies the good and bad with its head held high,
The flame that illuminated everything around,
Even darkness gives in wherever the flame is found,
Be the shining star, the irreplaceable kind,
Be the believer and let the heart not always rule the mind.

20

One Day at a Time

Whatever goal we are striving for, however rugged may be the climb,

We were certain to get there by putting in one day at a time,

The past may seem disturbing and the future far away,

Every new dawn gives us a chance to prove something to ourselves each day,

Forever is hard to imagine, and the future unpredictable as the passing breeze,

Some moments that make our heart smile and some in pain freeze,

A will is important in order to find a way,

Because no moment of life is here to stay.

21

Gifts of Nature

I sit in solitude among the lovely gifts of nature,
Admire everything so beautifully molded by the divine creator,
The green fields endlessly stretching together,
Admire the kingfisher gracefully drop a feather,
The clouds that slowly break themselves apart,
The cold wind flowing, memories fill the heart,
The train approaching between the gigantic trees on both sides,
Looking like the king of the field, showing off its might with full pride,
A cow grazing in the field far away,
The farmer chasing the notorious children, who spoil his bundle of hay,
Finally I see the sun settling down, As if the sky was wearing a crown ....

22

The Fear

I sat alone in my room all night,
When a sudden cacophony made the heart jump in fright,
A call, a cry for someone but the voice did not come out,
The blink of an eye and darkness all about,
Not a thing to be seen not a sound to be heard,
Like a disease which could not be cured,
When one is scared to take a step forward or move back,
As if heavens would fall and the earth would crack,
Gathering all the courage, I stumbled and fell,
Hit my head as if I had fallen into a deep dark well,
Once again the heart sank in fright,
But this time it was nothing but the flickering of the the tube light,
The fear was nothing but a bad dream,
Amazing how real imagination can seem ...

23

Someone

Someone we deeply care for,

Someone we always want to be there for,

A smile as soothing as walking on a bed of the petals of roses,

Someone whose thoughts fill the heart when in the silver night the eye closes,

Someone who most preciously in our heart we behold,

The warmth merely by the emotions that help to beat the cold,

The enchanting feeling of listening to the waves,

Someone, somewhere that the heart always craves ...

24

I Stand Still in Reverence as God is Standing By

I stand still in reverence as I look at the moving clouds in the sky,

I stand and admire the sun setting and know that lord is passing by,

Hands folded in obeisance I bow my head and pray to thee,

I thank him for everything I have and feel the presence next to me,

A belief that every situation is orchestrated by thee,

One should hear his name resounding in every word and pray for union with thee.

25

Over the Hill and Far Away

Over the hill and far away,

Lies a goal for which we strive each day,

One cannot determine the time it would take,

We move ahead trying, learning from mistakes,

There are times we sacrifice for reasons beyond comprehension,

Every effort seems in vain and aggravates the tension,

The journey to the goal every obstacle one would have to withstand,

Objectively deal with situations and try and understand,

When we try and earn the tune on something that we spend,

We have to keep in mind that it is the beginning never an end!

26

Friends

A friend is a person, who accepts you as you are,
In ones heart, near or far,
Bad friends are like dry straw that upon life's surface flow,
To find the true friends one must in the ocean of life dive deep below,
A true friend is like an oyster pearl, precious and rare,
Unlike appalling ones like lemon seeds no one can bear,
Bad friends like autumn leaves wither away,
But the good ones like the unshakable tree trunk are there to stay,
Aim for retaining the good ones as a relationship with time stronger grows,
However be careful as the serpent always lies under the rose.

27

Father

To describe my father I have no words,
To me he is like what feathers are to birds,
Without the support of feathers, birds can't fly,
With him by ones side, the limit is the sky,
A father who is truly a cut above the rest,
Humility of a saint, he only deserves the best,
Accepts mountainous challenges, like a soldier daring,
A heart full of love and ever caring,
When negativity takes over me like the weakening drug,
He encourages one to fold hands to the almighty above,
He makes life seems like a matter of choice,
With a positive attitude inside and an enlightening voice,
In the crossroads of life a sheath anchor and a best friend.

28

Mother

Mother, the guiding star of everyone's existence,
A shock absorber for all with an everlasting heartening persistence,
Like my mother's guardianship which can seldom go wrong,
When life seems to fall like a pack of cards, she holds ones hand steady and strong,
When life seems on the downward incline she clings on to us so near,
And turns into positivity each and every fear,
Sincerity and nobleness is like a mothers eternal rule,
A mother is truly one cannot mislead or fool,
She teaches us to conquer every battle that comes our way,
And keeps us away from all elements that may lure us in negative ways,
An irreplaceable asset, a mother is a best friend,
Who sticks by us from the time we are conceived till the very end ...

29

The Setting Sun

The sun slowly spreading gold sprinkles on the ocean bed,
As if in a mother's lap rests a child its head,
The moon that emerges like a silver coin and rises high,
One solemnly sits and admires the star studded sky,
And somewhere among those glittering stars,
We close our eyes and relive life's hours,
Count the blessings and time carries one through,
Situations in life one cannot undo,
Do not work on impulse; carefully tread the path from the start,
Keep a hold on the mind and the heart,
Take life as it comes and things will work out one sees,
We can only try and leave the rest to the almighty.

30

The Sea of the Heart

The sea of the heart, the many ripples of love,

The currents which grow stronger like a magnetic force from above,

In the moss of truth when the heart gets caught,

And the mind preoccupies with endless thoughts,

Rough tides like an ongoing trial that test ones belief,

Facts of life hard as the coral reef,

Purity of the soul, like someone walked in without a sound,

Like someone came n one feels spellbound,

A symbol of eternity,

A true feeling that sets one free...

31

The Art of Being

When someone inspires your existence to the very core,
A master in disguise like the lord deep within we store,
One wonders who you owe the honor to,
Like an invisible hand which has always carried
you through,
Like the creepers which over a period of time intertwine,
Like a rainbow which is stirred by the sunshine,
Graceful as the flying birds yet with a determination
so strong,
A conviction that withered every storm,
A smile which leaves the heart enchanted,
A look at the face is like every wish by the almighty is granted ...

32

The moon – A Best Friend

One talks to the moon as if during the long dark night it were a best friend,

A strong bond which would under no circumstance end,

I wonder how it must be to be surrounded by the shining stars,

Like the king of a castle it stands majestic for hours,

During the anxious night, it even has a smiling face,

As if asking the heart and mind to stop the endless race,

Eyes closed, the mysticism surrounds me and every time I look at the moon,

As if it were looking right back to promise that with the answers it will be beside soon ...

33

The Rolling Ball of Life

Abilities in us are like natural plants,
Gifts from the almighty, special grants,
We are able to focus on the "being" if we really are,
Let the karmas be priority and always at par,
For nurturing one's ability one must be mentally stable,
Wings of the intellect and emotion one must enable,
Explore full potential and pursue them all,
The beauty about life is that it is like a rolling ball.

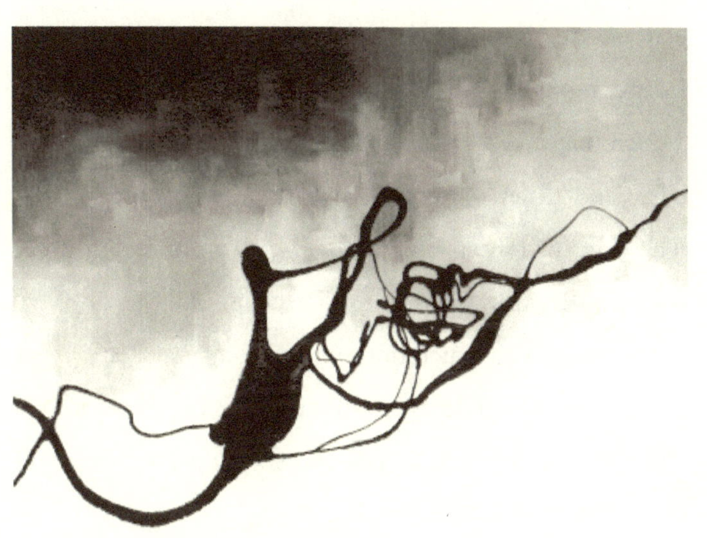

34

The Morning Glory

Early in the morning when the sun comes out,

Scattering its warmth all about,

I open the window for a breath of fresh air,

The wind blows a melody as if you were right there,

The chirping birds dispersing music all around,

Like a Sufi was in your reflection spellbound,

A compassion to which nothing can compare,

A loss of words to describe what one emotionally bears,

Till the flower of my soul withers, my love for you will remain,

I want my smile to substitute your every pain ...

35

Flower Seeds

Scattered like the dry flower seeds,
Which eventually to lovely blossoms lead,
Like a spiritual connection so divine,
A heart that beats to the rhythm of mine,
An individual full of love who sustains oneself,
In the glory of whom many dwell,
Distinction bestowed upon this person so treasured,
The value of who cannot be measured.

36

Came, Conquered and Stayed

A determination of the heart and the mind,
Accompanied by a sentiment, unexplainable and tough to find,
A sealed emotion somewhere deep inside,
An existing belief, eyes that in the shadowy night cried,
Faith, stronger than the possession of wealth and power,
Optimism like a candle ablaze in the cold heaven shower,
No religious affair that put the soul at ease,
No certainty that would let the hope increase,
And yet you emerged on a moonlit night,
Like waking up from a dream that revealed you in sight,
A thousand battles were conquered between the spirit and soul,
And your image close to my heart I behold......

37

When

When you walked into my life,I found a friend in you,

And now together hand in hand we make our dreams come true,

A look on your face with the warm embrace,

Because of which I feel any hindrance I could face,

Love consists of a power where two become one,

One never feels lonesome and yet sometimes mentally secluded among everyone,

Faithfulness like a connection between one and the supreme,

The reality of love which is better than any dream.

38

Awakening

An awakened state of mind, like the fragrance of fresh flowers

Love like meditation turns positive every hour,

The game of life which complicates the mind,

And in the vein of the body a battle we find,

A force which guides one to an everlasting energy unknown,

Like a seeker who looks for a path in the depth of spiritual being,

All that one has is faith in the power unseen,

An emotions that penetrates the core and an awakening one feels,

Love which so many secrets unveils.

In a moment one feels the joy of the countless fears,

All the happiness is liberated which was cocooned for the past years.

39

Enchanted

Like the loyalty of the sun every dawn,
The melodious jingle of birds singing,
The freshness of the dew on blades of wet grass,
The blossoming of the vibrant flowers,
The softness of the feather of a bird,
The mystic sensation in the heart in the drizzling cold weather,
As if in the middle of wilderness where not a soul is around,
Enchanted in the thoughts of someone, spellbound,
A reflection in the mirror of life, like a magnetic force,
This over a period of time inevitably grows.

40

Life – A Chase

Sometimes the chase of life one cannot understand,
Circumstances break us like an overstretched rubber band,
Drowned in the ocean of existence inexplicable thoughts,
Like to the questions of life, answers no one has got,
One quarrels with loved ones and knows not why,
A smile on the face sometimes we want to cry,
We look debatably at the moon n stars,
The loss of someone we assumed was eternally ours,
What we have we must truly cherish,
Because at the blink of an eye it can perish,
'If we hurt someone, one must let the ego bend,
Let the emotional quotient take over and the bitterness end,
Time is a big healer and always carries one through,
Just focus on the karmas in all you do.

41

Miles, Milestones... Missing

When we miss someone, separated by miles we are,
And yet they seem like every breathe we take each second of every hour,
The boundaries seem eternal sometimes fill our eyes with tears,
Even though you have them, there is something the heart fears,
Meeting someone is destiny; falling in love is like quicksand,
Emotions undivided, like a perpetual dreamland,
We believe we are immune to emotions and yet forever seems too less,
To let them know what we feel for them no words can express,
The flicker of the candle light when the wind blew so strong,
And yet it stood determined as love like there was an unseen bond,
Love, the constant source of joy and pain,
As beautiful as the rainbow on a sunny day when it rains,
As impossible as it is to finding a teardrop in the ocean is to let them know,
The solitude remained in the crowd the day away they decided to go

42

Flickering Candle

I close my eyes and see a white light with a candle flickering in the storm,

Fighting to remain lit as if to be a winner it were born,

Every time the storm grew violent the candle flickered brighter,

As if it were telling the wild storm that it were born to be a fighter,

The depth of the turquoise oceans, like the anonymity of life,

The cold wind blowing, tears turn into ice,

You wait, hope and long that one day you wake up and say,

The battle is over now, finally I live life my way,

The white light remains and the candle is still lit,

The storm only makes it stronger and more determined bit by bit

43

The Path

The pathway of life is merely what we want for it to be,
The silver line is upon us to pursue and see,
We envision several things in life,
But in introspect wonder if for them we really strive,
Overcoming inhibitions to really live a dream,
In real life situations impossible it seems,
Various aspects that obstruct the peace of mind,
Often walking the path in a dilemma ourselves we find,
Listening to the voice of the silence in the head,
As if one felt the emotions with nothing being said,
The addictive thought process, with which we follow the path,
No end to this mayhem, a vicious circle from the start.

44

Happiness

Philophies that one tries to follow,

Seeking happiness within when situations feel hollow,

One actively pours what one has within,

The line between the truth n disillusions seems very thin,

A powerful state which leaves one daydreaming,

Tears with laughter and joyfully screaming,

One must back up the mind with a positive conviction,

Let complexities not lead the heart into friction,

Be inspired, enjoy every moment of living,

Be attracting the right forces of the universe and in turn happiness will be given.

45

Mental Cultivation

Thoughts that trigger so many emotions,
We live our lives by pre conceived notions,
Mental cultivation that is often perplexed,
Entwined within like a vicious web,
Follow the craft of compassion in all we do,
Humble and let the karmas carry one through,
The drowsiness which takes over boundless like the sky,
Emotions which are of the mind passersby,
A mental equilibrium one must envision to attain,
A condition which only with positivity one can gain

46

Synchronicity – EQ and the IQ

Sometimes we let the Ego take the better of a situation,

We lose the ability to assess our emotions,

A turmoil within hence we take everything in a negative light,

Sadness takes prominence and of the ray of optimism we lose sight,

And then someone comes along,

As if a tune was incorporated in a meaningless song,

The mind and eart finally feel in sync,

As if a dry pen was suddenly filled with ink,

The emotion and intellect walk hand in hand,

Like one finally got what was lost in life's unpredictable quicks and...

47

As Precious as Pearls in the Ocean Deep

Like a beautiful dream which makes me want to not wake up from sleep,

As rare as a shooting star falling mysteriously from the sky,

As majestic as the mountain high,

Every sorrow you turn into a reason to smile,

With you it seems easy to walk the difficult mile,

A blessing which so close to my heart I behold,

Unveiled to me by lord like a secret untold,

I would run out of words if to your value I had to put a price,

You bring happiness to my soul and in you in where my faith lies...

48

Eternal Faith

Love which gives the strength that the best is still ahead,
A relationship like the needle and thread,
The tenderness of a touch like a mother to her child,
Like a striking rose which grows in the wild,
The finest chapters of life, filled with you,
An eternal faith which carries one through,
When someone has the ability to accept another with all faults,
A glance and all obstacles halt,
An anchor to ones ship, a cut above the rest,
A shining star in the sky of life, better than the best.

49

Sometimes in Life

Sometimes in Life we sit back and think,
How enigmatically we find someone and develop a link,
An inexpressible value of someone in mind,
A loss of words, nothing appropriate that can define,
As if they have remained close to one, near or far,
And the significance has amplified each passing hour,
As if lord bestowed a blessing in disguise,
A never-ending saga in the mystery called life.

50

Conciousness

We often refer to a sense of consciousness in living,
Mental and Physical state which is present in every being,
Each directly proportionate to the other,
Imperative as without one no sense can blossom further,
As individuals we are bound to live in delusion and ignorance,
It is hard to tune the mind to acceptance,
Time is a teacher which uncovers the deepest levels of the consciousness,
A state which has no boundaries and is timeless,
A karmic retribution, the levels unidentified,
Meditation which many individuals have tried,
And as we are confronted with various philosophies of life,
To attain and maintain the consciousness we perpetually strive.

51

Impermanence of Life

Change is the only consistence factor of life they say,
Time that drifts uncontrollably every second of each day,
The origins of destiny which one cannot question only wonder,
A blink of an eye and things pass by like lightning and thunder,
The unchangeable supreme law orchestrated by a force unknown,
Various situation which to us by life are shown,
The only permanence of existence is the impermanence,
Because everything eventually dies down like a fragrance.

52

Night

Into the tender night, eyes gaze at the shadow far,
As it vanished slow n steady like a shooting star,
Arms wide open as if waiting to embrace,
The ever existing shadow moving with life's pace,
Like seagulls that know not the depth of the ocean wide,
And yet fly above so proudly taking the offerings of the tide,
The feel of the night like one was wrapped around in cotton,
Like the sight of a beloved's face where all else was forgotten,
The night which brings with it a feeling freedom from the daily dissension,
A joy felt in the heart which no words can describe or mention.

53

Flowers

So many emotions a flower indicates,

A smile among tears is what it creates,

The bloom that leads to memories galore,

Like the feeling of walking on a breezy day by the sea shore,

Fresh start, sometimes nostalgia it within,

The brightness and beauty which makes you disregard everything,

A flower shoulders duties in times of sorrow and elation,

Truly one of nature's best creations.

54

Silence

A state of bliss or maybe not,
Self absorption which not many individuals have got,
In the world of today where a race broods over every day that goes past,
Sometimes we hope for the silence to eternally last,
A ceaseless gush of feelings that one internally feels,
The noisiest situations, silence reveals,
When in the dart board of life one is constantly aiming to achieve,
The silence from meditation which we reinforce ourselves to believe,
As if silence also was a medium of articulation,
When we speak or close our eyes in meditation.

55

The Clock

A symbol of moving forward and time that remain still,
Unaffected by seasons, the master of no one's will,
Ticking away as a dutiful server,
Of every situation a keen observer,
An infinite significance, a nomad of sorts,
Unmoved by the circumstance destiny has brought,
A minor variation when the battery runs out,
A two-second job and the clock is up and about,
Priceless like a loved one's care,
No vacation for the clock which in every situation is there.

56

Within and Without

The solemnity of the ambience around,
Some self created some in which we are naturally bound,
A demolition within in a situation unexpected,
Some scars that for a lifetime leave us affected,
A feeling within, that we cannot live without,
An assurance and yet somewhere a spectacle of doubt,
A sense of connection without and within,
Wrapped in which is the very facet of every being.

57

Romance

Harmonious notes that strum when one looks at your face,
Like winning life's challenging race,
Like tulips and roses that soothe the soul,
In the realm of existence where the heart controls,
One reflects on what an individual means to you,
Emotions bounce rapidly in all you do,
The fragrance of romance, Sparkling eyes,
Exuberance which through the heart flies.

58

My Soulmate

No definition, no structure,no rules written,
Just the mere aura of someone and one is totally smitten,
Engulfed like a melodious tune that draws one near,
The crackling sound of fire, like burnt was every fear,
The perspective which alters the path of the mind,
In an individual, your soul mate one finds,
Like a sanity that helps you focus on the better aspects,
Like an umbrella which from the storm and rain protects,
A soul mate that is like the intoxicating vintage wine,
Addictive, no substitute to you one can find.

59

The Wilderness

The fields that cover miles of unexplored land,
The scarecrow which isolated among the fields stands,
The vernal breeze blows and i feel your presence my love,
The nightingale sings, like a message from lord above,
When the evening dark is dispelled and my heart engages in your thought,
The joy beyond comprehension which along with yourself you have got,
In the wilderness of the field every time i stood,
Arms and eyes wide open as if in a distance you stood,
I wished to sleep only because you would come into my dream,
And paradise everything around would seem.

60

Instinct

Aspects of life embodied in the soul,
"Instinct" an emotion beyond explanation or control,
Embodied inside the soul and mind,
A definition for the feeling hard to find,
Whether in delight or depressed,
An instinct cannot be internally suppressed,
A beauteous rose which proudly stands,
Sometimes have hurtful thorns, the pain hard to withstand,
An instinct in various shades of life is seen,
A part of every race it exists n in various circumstances is seen.

61

Miracle

Like a celestial awareness in the subconscious exists,
In the most hopeless situation a ray of hope it gives,
Many a time we are the victims of fate,
Like the lord had closed his eyes and heaven's gate,
And then one day amidst the grey clouds,
You hear the sound of the thunder loud,
Washes away the anxiety and all the pain,
The wait no more seems to be in vain,
A miracle for sure and that's when you accept,
That the individual is the biggest miracle you could get.

62

The Cage

Like you keep reaching out for something and it seems to go far,
Like at the blink of an eye vanishes the shooting star?
Like battling emotions inside with which you try and deal,
As if an everlasting memory of a movie reel,
Mental boundaries from which we try and escape,
Life could pass us by but it is never too late,
Feelings that keep flirting with the reality,
As if we have lost mental gravity,
One must from the cage consciously break free,
Because life still carries on no matter what the circumstance maybe.

63

Enthusiasm

An enthusiasm to live not just survive,
To take risks, like a still heart would suddenly come alive,
The internal revolution, where the individual tries to find,
The meaning of life, the balance between the heart and mind,
Simple occurrences which are governed by a mystic force,
A day to day battle that engulfs us like a drop in the sand,
Like scavengers we try and find our place on the land,
Beneath the surface where no person can tell,
Like throwing a coin in a wishing well,
Like fixtures in a daily chaos, constantly moving and yet an internal stall,
Almost like trying to segregate colours from the graffiti on the wall.

64

Detour

No direct route, no direction in sight,

No ray of hope, no guiding light,

A constant discovery, solitary detention,

The ecstasy and agony of love and sadness,

The mental and emotional detours that make one feel an undefined madness,

We wake up each morning but may not be fully awake,

A detour which from within something shakes,

No motivation, no meditation helps us come out,

The voice in our head which constantly shouts,

The detour, mostly beyond ones control,

Memories and moments which in our heart we withhold.

65

The Beat of the Raindrops

The Rhythm of the breeze which flows at its will,
Makes the trees n flowers sway when they are still,
The rhythm of the rain that evokes so many emotions,
Like the drops wash away so many in built notions,
The way the drops of rain avalanche down ones face,
Like a friend who hides one's tears in a secure place,
The toddler that wades in the splashes of collected,
The lovers heart which watching the rain got affected,
The drizzle which left the rhythm of the heart dance,
Always takes one into an undefined trance.

66

The Potrait

The gazing eyes behind the glass,
From the ancient time, a message trying to pass,
A kind face with an expression hard to explain,
As if trying to camouflage some sort of wound or pain,
A well-crafted modesty almost captured in that art,
And yet flamboyancy like that of a child's heart,
I touched the portrait as if it were speaking to me,
I close my eyes and think of thee,
We are like that portrait enraptured in the glass frame,
Liberated from within and yet so mentally restrained.

67

Shielding Power

A power that all of us need to live in the world of today,
Negative forces that take over by forces that influence our night n day,
A shielding power through which no one can penetrate,
To keep pessimism away, like a sturdy indestructible inner gate,
The ability to resist the negative vibe,
Focus on the positive, take life in ones stride,
The essence of the marvellous power internally engraved,
A Self inspired drive that cannot be swayed,
Keep your deeds right as karma comes around,
The almighty settles the scores without a sound.

68

The Confrontation

The Confrontation, a topic of disturbance and fear,
Matters of the mind but the heart is too near,
A landslide of thoughts in the mountain of the human darkness,
Where so many strings we try and harness,
Continuity in the human action,
Unanswered questions, to some no reaction,
Existence seems obligatory, sometimes no sense it makes,
Drained our emotionally, so much energy life takes,
The constant confrontation between the spirit and the mind,
A lifetime spent to define the mantra, often hard to find.

69

The Feeling of Feeling

In the depths of memory your name i chanted,
When u left as if the last wish to lord was not granted,
Deathlike still, tears that in the cold wind froze,
All that remained were thorns in the stems of the Red Rose,
The countless ways to deal with the ache,
Numbness took over like a punishment for an unforgivable mistake,
Clad in the grey clouds were the sun and skies,
Clipped were the wings of the bird that determinedly flies,
A wish in the heart, one strung together the necklace of hope,
When everyone said there was no point or scope,
And when you stood before me i realised there was never a farewell,
Because in you i have been bound in an everlasting spell.

70

The Droplets of Water

Droplets of water that caress the cheeks,
As if a language of their own they speak,
When a loved one manages to tremble the emotional wellness inside,
For the one you have stayed up, laughed and cried,
A helpless feeling, like a lump in the throat,
Like isolated in the ocean, in a sinking boat,
The one close to you just leaves you to be,
No droplet they care for, no emotion they see,
And that's when you realise that the droplets are no one's but your own,
A return present for all the love you have shown.

71

Truth

Facts in which we like to believe
Notions which every moments our mind conceives,
The numerous debates that go on in our head,
On the fine line of conscience on which as individuals we tread,
Principles and Ethics, to which we are forced to submit,
The real essence of the truth in our soul is not lit,
The hypocrisy which delimits the mind,
And in meditation the truth one tries to find,
A state of awareness which we pass through every day,
Like trying to find thread in a stack of hay.

72

The Dialogue

Sandwiched between the heart and mind the dialogue persists,
As if two individuals with differences co-exist,
The dialogue where the mind speaks and the heart feels,
The good sense which sometimes the psyche steals,
Finding the normality in life like a fantasy of its own,
Anxiety which sometimes beyond evaluation has grown,
The maze of emotions, even though the laughs around are broad,
One feels astray within, looks up at heaven to ask lord,
And we speculate what we are filling up in life's mystifying bottomless pot,
Star gaze, ponder over what we do have and have not.

73

The Beginning of Togetherness

Beyond the limit of the skies when the heart starts to beat,
One glance at the person and life seems so complete,
One feels if the mountain crumbles down, one wouldn't care,
To save the treasured one from the hailstorm every confrontation of life one would bear,
Every breath that one takes is committed to the one we so exceedingly care for,
To them we could dedicate the existence the only reason we are there for,
As if the beginning of infitinity, an exploration of a nature,
Where the only orchestrator is the mighty creator.

74

My Classical Theme – The One I Love

To me you are as distinctive as a classical theme,
Timeless like philosophy, a depiction of the most wonderful dream,
Like the true voice of an inner calling, identification with devotion,
A glimpse of you my the treasured one, and flies away every pessimistic notion,
The strong sentiment one feels for you is afar from explanation,
As if a blind person was suddenly able to see lord's creation,
The courage that you give to be a fighter in the battlefield of life,
The conviction with which for the goal you strive,
A look at your beaming eyes and one feels internally complete,
Because you are the name that resounds in my every heartbeat.

75

The Saga

The circle of life, a saga which each day continues,
The intent of life which is sometimes by us misconstrued,
Every morning awakened by the chirping birds and hawkers calling,
Look out of the window, a child off his bicycle falling,
The coffee mug which so patiently waits,
The newspaper man stands smiling at the gate,
A bunch of ladies at a distant stand,
Almost seem like a wedding band,
The fragrance of detergent, the whistle of the cooker,
A pigeon in the balcony as an everyday onlooker,
The saga of life, a revelation each instant,
A steady reminder that in life change is the only constant.

76

A Force

Forces and the energies of the universe which words fail to explain,

The rationale for joy and the incomprehensible one for pain,

Like one was encapsulated in the force which almost feels real,

As if possessed by an unnatural energy, something so surreal,

Trying to reach out to the mirage which one can see,

How delusional, how deceiving nature can be,

Something that does not exist seems to be in sight,

As if to something we are so morally bound,

In an individual the forces of the universe we found,

Contentment in the love as if we found the most powerful force of them all,

As if the revolving earth suddenly came to a stall.

77

Survival of the Pursuit

The importance of a goal in life is indefinable,
Situations in life which blur the vision which we try and keep stable,
The ladder of life which we climb with so many factors that co-exist,
Life may drop us unaware and yet for an answer we unconsciously insist,
Sometimes on a mere Ego on we we try and thrive,
Self awareness gets dissolved inside and we struggle for it to survive,
The pursuit is what remains, even forgetting what we are pursuing,
Losing track of the purpose and the meaning of what we are doing,
A strange factor is this pursuit that is always a part of our core being,
Sometimes misguiding us as we overlook the obvious which we are seeing,
And in joy and sorry all that survives is the pursuit,
Even when we avoid a situation the "pursuit" asks us to do it.

78

The Tree

It stands in solitude weathering many a storm,
Moments that turns to dusk and the ones that turn to dawn,
On a mountain top where no one goes it stands and awaits,
The cold passing icy wind and yet it stands straight,
A passerby stops to take a nap and under its canopy it protects,
Even though in return not a thank you note it gets,
The older it gets the more it droops but the conviction remains strong,
As if the wait was eternal, like an umbilical cord bond,
Many lovers scribble their name on it, thinking it will never die,
As if it were a everlasting as the moon n sun in the sky,
Many roles that it plays, many years that it takes in,
No discrimination towards anyone, protecting everything.

79

The Crowd

The inexplicable nature of the feeling with which one is always surrounded,

An invisible knot with which the heart is always grounded,

An argument inside, a reflection at a distance not so far,

The affirmation in the nature of life which is always at par,

Sometimes one feels like they are losing grip, as if turned blind,

The crowd, in which oneself we cannot find,

The constant seek of rationality, recurring situations of living,

Some incidents which are hurtful and beyond forgiving,

The crowd that drowns one, and u feel like a string less kite,

As if a bird without feather, sits still in fright,

And then in the crowd there comes a face,

The reason for illumination at every dark corner of the place.

80

The River of Faith

The elusive concepts on the river of belief,

Solidify over time like the coral reef,

Formless and yet so sturdy and glitter,

Ripples of emotion that on the stream of faith are littered,

The endless philosophies of life which we raft upon,

A blink of an eye and far away they are gone,

The fantasies that last, the realistic side that stays,

The swiftness with which moments turn into days,

It is like trying to hold onto a shadow, adaptation being key,

Like listening to the sound of silence, questioning thee,

Trying to figure out the central truth, we cruise alongside the river,

Rock solid at times and the trying situations where life wakes one up with a quiver.

81

The Pattern of Life

The blueprint of life that gets affixed in a definite mould,
No warning signs, no scripts that are pre-determined or told,
The survival, derivation and many questions profound,
The banter in the head like empty vessels being thrown around,
Some chapters we fill with people, who live unfilled scars,
For the one we spent in laughter and pain one too many hours,
The patterns changes, the basic theme remain the same,
A song that reminds us of the walk in the directionless lane,
We learn to make peace and carry on with the ever-changing pattern,
The conglomeration of the various aspects inexplicable by any study of any religion.

82

The Wait is Eternal

A wait that is eternal, a wait unknown,
The wait which has remained, an anxiety which over a period of time has grown,
A face, the outline like around the dark cloud is seen,
The past, the present, even a part of the future unseen,
A faded voice across the mountain high,
A collision of feelings, like getting drenched by the waves splashing by,
A silent cry lost in the stormy night so dark,
Of the burning flames all that remain are sparks,
The everlastingness of the feeling, no definitive formulation to the wait,
Like in a constant magical, hypnotized state.

83

Only if

Only if i could let you know,
That it was not me who had let go,
I waited long, with a longing heart and damp eyes,
Hoping that you would hear the cries,
It was only the distance but would have been alright,
If you had with the same enthusiasm support the fight,
And then one day there came a day,
We were lost somewhere along the way,
If only you knew of the endless starts ive counted,
Of the memories which i was constantly haunted,
All that remained is the wish that you understood,
And we would never fall apart, fighting the odds as hard as we could.

84

Attitude

A double-faced word, the implication so strong,
Sometimes depicting the right, and at times atrocious and wrong,
It exists in every individual good or bad,
It is the string attached to the happy and sad,
It enhances our thinking depending upon the situation at the time,
A sequence of thoughts depending on the attitude we hold,
Leading to consequences that one cannot pre define?
A factor of life which by many aspects is controlled,
It is important to have one in life as it carries you far,
Just be sure when to use it, let not the mind always overrule the heart and be at par.

85

The Imagination

The imagination of a world where just love and compassion exist,

No fears, no preconceived notions or the standard checklist,

A rainbow which fills the canvas of the sky with elation,

One of lord's most mysterious creations,

A sensation at the mere thought that crosses the mind,

And in another world ourselves we find,

Hoping that the "imagination" would turn into a fact,

Not just like a scene in life's long lasting act,

Something that cannot be perceived and yet seems so true,

A part of everything in life we may or may not do.

86

Eternity

The everlastingness of a sensitivity one feels deep within,
Like a vicious circle like the inexplicable waves and tides,
Like antiquity, so precious and dearly possessed,
Like a miraculous feeling of unknowingly being blessed,
Eternity a word that depicts the endless facts and fears,
Far away and yet so near,
A word which conquers both living and dying,
Beyond our control, all we can do is keep trying,
The eternal waves of time that engulf our being,
Accepting them unknowingly and sometimes the brutal truth seeing,
Not an option in life as the word rules over time,
Turbulence where we fall off the cliff and sometimes all seems perfect fine.

87

Ancient Thoughts

Ancient thoughts resound with echoes of the unknown,
A blend of various emotions which the mirror of the heart to us has shown,
An appearance of someone who like an angel come into sight,
Tearing its way like through the dark cloud a ray of light,
With utmost grace the person walks right in,
Like being awakened to a dream where perfect is everything,
But then the ancient thought make us drift away,
An unknown land,we feel internally astray,
But the only reality is that we are compelled to accept,
As if paying some unidentified debt,
Ancient thought for a lifetime remain,
Leaving us happy and sometimes helpless in vain.

88

The Wait Was Not Enough

Like i walked the moon and lived floating in the air,

The presence i felt like you were right there,

The relationship was over but the commitment remained,

The bitterness of the cold nights which the heart sustained,

I talked to you in my dreams and said,

Always tied strongly with you with an unseen thread,

Reached out for the rose and welcomed by a bee sting.
Seemed deserted the flowers of spring,

And all i ever thought was the wait is never enough,

It was merely a situation, life was being rough,

And one day the dry flower petals were blessed with morning dew,

The wait was for the best thing emerged in the form of you.

89

Randomness – Emotions in Motion!

Random thoughts like pulling flowers off the garden green,
Suddenly magnificent seems life's theme,
The bamboo shoots that spread positive around,
Motionless feelings in which the heart is unconsciously bound,
The numberless times we promise our self,
The countless memories which each day we try and shelf,
Sometimes the distressful tears of sorrow remain,
Uncalled for incidents that revives the settled pain,
The meter of life that keeps ticking away,
Times that one is totally grounded and those completely astray.

90

The Abstractions of Life

The abstractions of life that reflect in the everyday living,
Infinite surprises that life keeps on giving,
An abstract self consciousness in which we are tightly clasped,
Social critiques which keep us constantly grasped,
Neutrality which we try and attain,
A constant racket between the loss and gain,
The expanding complexities and the contradictions attached to it,
Like trying to solve a mathematical abstraction bit by bit,
And various formulas we try to solve the fractions Dealing with life's law of mental and spiritual attraction.

91

Infinite Spaces

The various dimensions of the mind,
Imprisoned in infinity we find,
Situations good and bad that awaken us to things,
Directly proportionate to our core being,
Like the mind was uplifted into an infinite breathing space,
Where angels exist and peace exists in every place,
An individual who walks in and beautifies the grandeur of the soul,
Fills the space delightfully with feelings hard to control,
A positive force all around, an explanation hard to give,
And with that individual in the infinite space for a lifetime we decide to live.

92

The Internal Pilgrimage

Sitting in mental solitude, sensing the vibes around,
An internal state of ecstasy when the spirit is drowned,
Like the presence of holiness, an inner exploration,
A goal towards which we move with full determination,
A key examination of what we feel,
So many things which under the layers of emotion we conceal,
Motives, conviction and a new significance to the search,
Like a loved one put an end to the very long lasting complicated research.

93

The Droplet of Water

The droplet of water on the window pane,
Through the storm patiently on the glass it remains,
Trickles down as the wind blows in the direction of the drop,
As if listening to instructions it suddenly stops,
When we touch it, a part of it vanishes in thin air,
A glimpse of the eye and it seems to be right there,
A comparison to life which can slip away like the droplet,
The uncertainty to what in life we get,
Life, like the river downstream, we like the droplet small,
Sometimes turn into vapour and at others come to a stall.

94

The Images in My Mind

Even though time tore us apart,

You remained seated at the very bottom of my heart,

Vivid memories of the many nights,

Fragrance of fresh flowers with your thoughts were blooming bright,

The television channels that i surfed and stopped at a song,

That was a favourite of yours i missed you and sang along,

I would think of our first meeting and a smile across my face,

Your name echoing in the burning wood of the fireplace,

The many long walk with hail sparkling on the ground,

In every snowflake your image i found,

Even forever seems less now that my dream the heavens have shown,

For you i have and will cover innumerable milestones.

95

The Garden

At a distance stands a tree so tall,
Withered in many a storm and the winter fall,
Serene as if it has made peace with the heat,
A place where people in different situations meet,
No discrimination for the people, who in the garden sit,
In the brightness of the day and when the night is moonlit,
The blades of grass with many shades,
The garden that welcomes one and all,
The old man with the stick and the child with the ball,
No discrimination in which it lets everyone be a part of its space,
Trampled over each day and yet calmness on its face.

96

The Translation – Life

Like life was a different language we perpetually try and translate,
To words which we can understand and relate,
Like a collection of literature from the ancient times,
We spend each moment trying to make sense of the lines,
A vicious circle of humour and seriousness,
Amusing us with its enormity and wittiness,
Miracles and sometimes surprises we find objectionable,
The translation which we may at times find incomprehensible,
We sit in solitude and try reflecting,
Why the literature seems so perplexing,
But eventually it all starts making sense,
And life is filled with a smell of addictive fragrance.

97

Endlessly Drifting

Concealed inside the oyster in the ocean,
Focusing on external devotion,
A hostage to the many around us, putting behind all of one's needs,
Belonging to the universe and carrying out all deeds,
A subtle sacrifice in the name of love,
As if the wings were clipped off a dove,
Secret voices that in the head that relentlessly speak,
Giving one strength and sometimes regretful and weak,
The Endless drifting, a flashlight that awakens us inside,
And we learn to accept life's erratic ride

98

Soundless Water in the Depth of the Sea

Life which is sometimes soundless like the water in the deep sea,

Encapsulated are the countless beings which exist inside and we let them be? We go calmly among the racket and rush,

Sometimes getting drowned by the waters gush,

An emotional trance which a loved one makes us feel,

And every apprehension and anxiety is automatically healed,

Like wind chimes dancing away in the falling rain,

Like someone walked in with a magical touch and took away all the Pain,

Life feels calm like the soundless depths of the ocean,

And in control seems like every notion.

99

The Highway – Back to You

So many twists and turns that came and went,
Winds that carried floating petals that left your scent,
Many pebbles in the silent lake that i threw,
Taming the sorrows which in your absence grew,
In the god forsaken woods with an outstretched hand,
Snowflakes falling and in your thoughts i would stand,
The highway which i knew would lead back to you someday,
Sincerity in the soul which was there to stay,
Like an epic tale which would ultimately come alive,
Focussed when the only way to acquire is strive,
I knew sooner or later the highway will make way to you,
Because the adoration has been inexpressible and so true.

100

Dreaming a Dream

I dream of colours that exist not,
In this crowded place, my dream is all i have got,
I dream of a tune that is self-created,
A signal, for which forever i have waited,
A beating heart, an unknown space,
Hope that the dream in reality i face,
When i feel i am losing certainity,
I dream of a voice that reassures me,
I stand resolutely against what i feel is not just,
I dream that is my purpose and i absolutely must,
The various aspects of existence woven together,
As if the dream in the whirlwind was floating like a feather,
Watching the distant skies,often pondering over my dream,
Incomprehensible and yet like my shadow it seems.

101

From Us to You

As precious as pearls in the ocean deep,
Like a beautiful dream which makes me want to not wake up from sleep,
As rare as a shooting star falling mysteriously from the sky,
As majestic as the mountain high,
Every sorrow you turn into a reason to smile,
With you it seems easy to walk the difficult mile,
A blessing which so close to my heart I behold,
Unveiled to me by lord like a secret untold,
I would run out of words if to your value I had to put a price,
You bring happiness to my soul and in you in where my faith lies...

102

Nostalgia

Nostalgia that often clouds one's mind,

In a strange spot ourselves we find,

Silhouettes that make us feel astray,

Like a shadow that lingers behind us every moment of the day,

As if we are living in an unrealistic realism,

Memories locked away in the soul prison,

A feeling that makes one wants to dash across empty places
Eyes closed and the silhouettes turn into unidentifiable faces,

And then a look at someone worth the universe so wide,

An answer to all prayers ones lifelong joy and pride.

103

Sun Ablaze

A silent morning with the sun ablaze,
A heart full of memories, a mind in daze,
The cup of coffee to awaken the sense,
The distant mirage, like gods own lens,
As i watch the bird sipping water from the puddle,
Like a message which leaves the mind no more in a muddle,
The labour working to earn his bread in the heat,
Exhausted and yet the spirit no one can beat,
It is amazing how miraculous is the power within,
Makes us withstand the worst that nature has to bring,
Leaves me saying a prayer as i walk away with the glass,
As a hear a voice resound that this too shall pass...

104

The Dialogue

Sandwiched between the heart and mind the dialogue persists,
As if two individuals with differences co-exist,
The dialogue where the mind speaks and the heart feels,
The good sense which sometimes the psyche steals,
Finding the normality in life like a fantasy of its own,
Anxiety which sometimes beyond evaluation has grown,
The maze of emotions, even though the laughs around are broad,
One feels astray within, looks up at heaven to ask lord,
And we speculate what we are filling up in life's mystifying bottomless pot,
Star gaze, ponder over what we do have and have not.

105

Unveiled

As precious as pearls in the ocean deep,
Like a beautiful dream which makes me want to not wake up from sleep,
As rare as a shooting star falling mysteriously from the sky,
As majestic as the mountain high,
Every sorrow you turn into a reason to smile,
With you it seems easy to walk the difficult mile,
A blessing which so close to my heart I behold,
Unveiled to me by lord like a secret untold,
I would run out of words if to your value I had to put a price,
You bring happiness to my soul and in you in where my faith lies...

106

We Live in a Cage

We live in a cage-confined mind, become a slave to our thoughts,

Alienate loved ones, sometimes don't respect what we have got,

In the road of life, we live with the word "beware",

Lessons unlearnt, we take for granted and are unaware,

Life chases us on tiptoe and we debate about love, if and why,

We talk about unpredictability but don't express and sit and cry,

Every cloud of dust that rises some of us have the ability to clear our eyes and pass,

We seek joy in the moonlit night and contentment from a patch of dew-drenched grass,

Absorbed in our dreams and yet not deceived, we live in a practical reality of our own,

Sensibility intact and yet eccentricity which over a period of time has only grown.

107

Instant

Like the voice of an angel, that in the subconscious lives,
Direction in an unknown world it gives,
Like standing in the middle of colliding mountains tall,
Like life was rolling down on a steep slope like a ball,
A note of a music chain that seems broken,
As if words too many were left unspoken,
Sometimes waking up in a fear that this might be it,
Seems like the wings of time were not letting the soul sit,
The reason for happiness is a person, who comes along,
Who seems to make sense of every unfinished note in the song,
A undeviating growth in love with every instant earned,
You are the icon from whom so much I've learned,
I know sometimes i crumble to the ground,
Just know that you are the most invaluable treasure in life i have found....

108

Love Oneself

Personality, Image, Etiquette or Style,
In order to enhance we must walk the extra mile,
Discover Your inner self and work towards building the blocks,
A Power within each one of us have got,
Each waking day is an opportunity for us to enhance,
As every new day is a beginning, a chance,
Start from the core and bear in mind there is always hope,
For improving the quality of existence there is forever scope,
Empower yourself and let no obstacle come your way,
Be unsinkable and develop yourself every passing day.

109

Voice Within

A guide through day and night,
An inner voice to clear the goal in sight,
Everyone needs a guide, our own best friend,
Who would help us through till the very end,
Amidst the holler we have to learn to stay still,
The only focus should be to be strong at the will,
The stagger along the way makes us grasp what matters,
Even though in certain situation the heart shatters,
An inexplicable empowerment comes when we start listening to our inner voice,
One rises above the shadows of time and understands that life is a matter of choice,
Once we start shedding destiny's layers,
We automatically conquer all our fears.

www.ingramcontent.com/pod-product-compliance
Lightning Source LLC
LaVergne TN
LVHW041110150826
845673LV00007B/1996

9798889098898